THE FONZ & HENRY WINKLER

His Real-Life Story Packed With Dozens Of Great Photographs

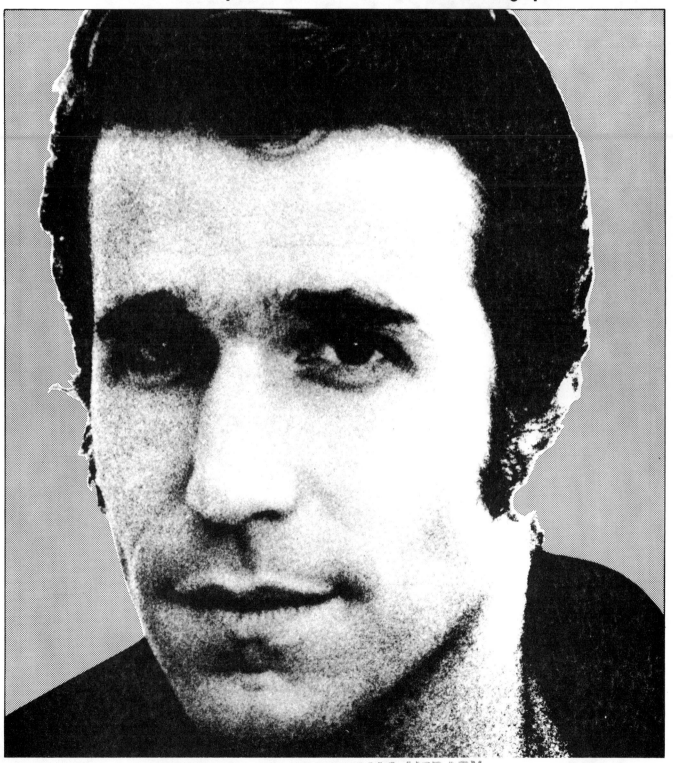

THE FONZ & HENRY WINKLER
By Jonathon Green

Book Designed by Michele Mortimer

We greatfully acknowledge the following photographic sources: London Weekend Television, Alan Band Associates, Trans World Features, Paramont Pictures Corporation, London Features, Keystone Press, Metromedia.

Packaged by H. Bunch Associates Ltd.
Published by Paradise Press, Inc.
Printed in the U.S.A.

A Bunch Books Package

CONTENTS

CHAPTER 1
IN THE BEGINNING

*"My first role was Little Tommy Toothpaste:
I screwed the cap off the top of my head,
squeezed my tummy and out came the
toothpaste – my tongue."*

In the beginning there were Harry and Ilse Winkler. Exiles from Hitler's Germany; Jews, naturally; well-to-do in the international lumber trade, more surprisingly. In 1939 they took the last Dutch boat from Amsterdam to New York. A few days later the Nazis took over. A few weeks later the Winklers, with thousands like them, were residents of New York City. In 1941 a daughter, Bea, was born. Four years later another child came home to the tenth floor apartment on 78th Street, in the heart of the city's middle class Upper West Side. His delighted parents named him for his grandfather, murdered in the death camps of Europe, and for the incumbent President of the United States. Henry Franklin Winkler, born October 30th, 1945.

Childhood for Henry Winkler was a fifties classic sure enough. But there wouldn't be any duck-tails for this youngster. Henry came from strictly the right side of the tracks. Father Harry had managed to launch as successful a business in the New World as he had left behind in the Old Country. His son was to be groomed for that business. He would learn the way the upper middle classes learnt. The natural progression of things, the knowledge of his place in the world — always up there at the top table. There was no poverty, no problems, no embryo juvenile delinquent in the making up there on W78th Street. The refridgerator was always full. There was even a governess — Nelly — who looked after Henry when his father was away on gruelling business trips and Ilse inevitably interested herself in the many community and charity organisations that provide the bedrock of Jewish New York.

Today Henry emphasises that the Winklers were never rich. Still, compared with the blacks, the Puerto Ricans, the rest of the multi-racial hotpot that makes up New York, there was no denying that they were comfortable. It was to show Henry the other side of that secure life that he was enrolled in P.S. 87, a run-of-the-mill public school where anyone and everyone learnt the basics of education. First came his primary school, Skytop Nursery School, where the actor to be created his first role as 'Toby Toothpaste': "In a memorable performance I screwed the cap off the top of my head, squeezed my little tummy and toothpaste (my tongue) came out of my mouth."

At P.S. 87 Henry set the educational standards that would stay with him for the rest of his career in schools and college — down there at the bottom of the class. Or somewhere thereabouts. Father Harry believed passionately in education. Son Henry fought his beliefs tooth and claw. "My father and I recreated the great battles of the world," Henry has said since, and the memory, while humorous, is tinged with the knowledge of just how bitter were those fights that pitted father against son. Fundamental beliefs against crazy-passionate optimism.

There were compensations, of course. Jerry Love, a friend of Henry's at both public school and beyond, remembers that he and the future star just "had a genuine good time". Henry was the class clown and soon learnt one of life's most important lessons, knowledge that experience and not schoolbooks gave him. The blissful high that comes from gaining centre stage with the audience baying for more. Maybe the teachers were less than enthusiastic, maybe Henry's parents studied his unimpressive report cards with stern and even disappointed faces, but Henry was having a great time. Academic plaudits could never hope to rival the gut pleasures that came from pleasing a crowd.

Childhood years passed by without any great excitement. Henry went to summer camp, like

every other middle class kid. He had a dog, whom he loved; played games with real friends — Leyland, with whom he concocted vile smelling chemical experiments — and imaginary ones — George The Horse, who acted as guru and confidant. He lost his tonsils and gained his ritual manhood at his Bar Mitzvah, the Jewish ceremony that makes thirteen year old boys into adults, mother permitting. The photos show cocky young Henry mugging with a candle in his mouth; the devout initiate reciting Hebrew texts — he reversed the order of the prayers and the rabbi made him start again — and the inevitable waltz with sister Bea while proud but nervous parents gyrate slowly alongside.

With Bar Mitzvah and its rituals came another, more substantial test. It was all fine to mix with the rest of the kids at P.S. 87 for those early years, but when it came to the tricky teenage years, then mixing with the masses was suddenly and certainly out of the question. New York has a number of private boys schools. Fee-paying parents expect, and generally get, a higher standard of teaching

than do their peers who opt to continue in public school. Like the British public schools, obstinately private in fact, these New York middle class academies were geared very much to success, and in particular the kind of success that led first to college and thence to an office desk.

Henry Winkler proved about as dud a pupil at McBurney, on New York's ritzy 63rd Street, as he had done at the less prestigious P.S. 87. Jerry Love again: "Neither of us was really — I don't think at any time — a crackerjack student. I suppose 'mediocre' would be the more appropriate word for our academic abilities." But, mediocre student or not, Harry Winkler had no intention of letting his less than academically inclined son just idle along at the bottom of the class. Henry was thirteen when he was sent for a term at the Lycee Jacard in Switzerland. The young man was already beginning to point out to his parents that his real ambition in life was the stage, but that cut no ice. Harry and Ilse were never anything but fond parents, still, they had their opinions on what their

only son was going to do and those opinions, they assured him, were the ones that counted. A good knowledge of French would help a career in an international firm, so off to Switzerland he would have to go.

Despite his misgivings, young Henry loved his time abroad. For a kid whose highest peaks had hitherto been the towers of the Manhattan skyline, the awesome Alps showed him how nature could put human endeavour to shame. Indeed, so impressed was Henry that he was dead set on climbing one of the peaks that could be seen from the Lycee's windows. Half-way up the mountain Henry got a little too sure and slipped. "I stepped on a loose rock, fell over backward and started tumbling down the steep slope. I flailed with my arms trying to grab something, but there was not a piece of shrubbery for we were far above the timberline. I'm not sure how far I fell . . . suddenly my hand closed on a small, scrawny tree, that had somehow managed to find a place to cling to on the rocks. That little tree saved my life." Miraculously Henry had survived his fall unhurt, but when he realised how near to death he had come "my

AAAAY! Its the man himself. Arthur Fonzarelli junior, the king of cool.

knees began shaking and didn't stop for a week".

Rock climbing disasters apart, Henry's time at the Lycee was a happy one. Even when the whole school looked like losing their holiday after the school bell went missing — Henry had hidden it and only when he returned it in a 'miracle discovery' were they let go — he was still enjoying himself. And back at McBurney Henry made up for his failings in the schoolroom with an increasing success among the teenage girls that he and his pals were pursuing. There wasn't a school dance that didn't see the budding Don Juan arrive with a sweet young thing on one or even both arms. Though the one-man double dates ended when one girl forced him to a tricky choice. When the decision went against her she was more than simply miserable. Her tears and entreaties made one thing clear to Henry: it was O.K. to play the field, but strictly one at a time. There was another drawback for Henry's dates. Chivalry wasn't exactly his strong point. Recalls Henry with a blush, "no sooner would we arrive at the dance than I'd be off mingling, leaving the poor girl trying to look poised

'Happy Christmas Fonzie' say this bevy of Yuletide beauties.

and cool in a roomful of people who were strangers to her". Still, even if Henry wasn't a knight in shining armour, it didn't seem to cramp his style; or his progress through the best looking girls around.

In all fairness to Henry, there was more to his days at McBurney than just clowning and kissing. Apart from a burgeoning acting career — of which more later — that went from strength to strength despite the disapproval of both his parents and the top drama coach, headmaster Dr. Quinn, Henry established an interest in the less privileged of his fellows. It has lasted to this day. In those days Henry worked after school as a counsellor at the Yorkville Youth Centre, a programme for under-privileged boys. Today, with his appearances in Telethons, his meetings with deprived and invalided children across the country, Henry Winkler is keeping up his good work.

As his final year at McBurney moved slowly towards graduation, Henry gained a place in Emerson College, Boston. It took a couple of tries at the exams — geometry proved especially intractable — but when the year ended and the graduation ceremonies moved to their conclusion, Henry could rest assured that the future was secure. And there was another important event that last summer at school, another type of graduation for which Henry had undoubtedly put in infinitely more dedicated preparation. "Shouldn't we get

undressed?" asked the girl. "Would you like me to leave the room?" replied Henry. Despite such unpromising preliminaries, Henry lost his virginity. "The telephone rang about an hour later. It was my sister. 'Why do you sound so funny?' she asked me. 'Give me a break, Bea, I can't talk to you now.' 'Do you have a girl in there?' . . ." Sure enough, Henry did and didn't mind telling his elder sister so. "Congratulations," she told him, "now get on with your maths homework!"

Then school was over and college lay enticingly in the distance. For his parents the future was still a cut and dried decision: young Henry, the son of their house, would be carrying on his father's business. No problems. For Henry Winkler, the plans were not so definite, and they were certainly not the same. Acting had gripped his ambitions. For years now the abilities and energy that might have gained him top marks had been diverted to a non-stop procession of stage success. Now there was college life, free of the restrictions that made school so boring and filled with all the potential that the young performer could desire. As he reminisced over that glorious afternoon of love in his parents' apartment, and daydreamed about the new term at Emerson College, Henry Winkler might not have been sure of what exactly the future had in store, but one thing was absolute: there was going to be plenty, and it would centre around the stage.

CHAPTER 2
STAGE STRUCK

*"I threw open the windows of my
apartment and yelled out to all of Boston
'I'm accepted at Yale!'"*

f there hadn't been a stage for him to act on, Henry Winkler would have had to have invented it. "I had done nothing but eat, drink and sleep theatre since the age of seven," Henry admits, "when I saw James Stewart in *Rear Window*. My feeling then was 'Wouldn't it be great to be able to do that'." A feeling that never left the ambitious youngster. A feeling that he will happily declare today is *still* a central motive in his whole acting career.

Stardom was still a long way off for the stage-struck seven year old. Though not as far as it might have seemed. Plenty of kids might have enjoyed watching all the glamour, excitement and dramatics of a live show, Henry made sure he was going to do something about it. From the thought to the deed can be a very long way, and that goes for the gap between the front stalls and centre stage too, but Henry was on his way. Ace student he might never claim to be; actor in the making, that was something very different.

Taking a look at Henry's fledgling performances, one thing stands out: it seems as if the talent that hundreds of millions appreciate today was just as certainly in evidence twenty years ago, if only for the pleasure of a lucky few. Aged fourteen he won his first real lead role Billy Budd in the play of the same name. "It was one of the proudest moments in my life." To celebrate the role, Henry bought a pair of black suede desert boots. He wore them, to the surprise of many patrons, throughout his performance as the hapless sailor.

With one role under his belt, Henry couldn't wait for the next. Yet despite his obvious abilities, his dramatic coach, McBurney's principal Doctor Quinn, was less than enthusiastic over his student's acting potential. Maybe it was Henry's lousy academic record that biased the principal, or

maybe it was just Quinn's bizarre obsession with knocking the talents of all his drama pupils, but as Jerry Love recalls, he really had it in for the young actor. "This Dr. Quinn would tell Henry, at every possible occasion, in the loudest voice, that he should direct his efforts somewhere else, because he was never going to make it as an actor, because he had no talent whatsoever." Huh! Today, there's no doubt, the misguided drama coach is eating his heart out, but back in 1959, his absurd attempts to undermine Henry had the force of any teacher reprimanding any student. Bar one thing: they didn't work. Henry is still intensely self-critical today, though that's probably more to do with his total professionalism than any seeds of misguided information sown by Dr. Quinn. But self-criticism is a long, long way from total resignation. If Henry puts in a performance that doesn't totally satisfy him, it doesn't mean that the *Happy Days* team are about to be minus one very important member. No way. It's just try harder to achieve that elusive standard of perfection next time.

Which is exactly the response that Henry had to anyone who tried to convince him that acting wasn't his future career. As the lead roles began to come his way, as first the school and then, reluctantly, his parents began to accept that this was not just another enthusiastic amateur but a performer of real depth and perception, Henry gained more and more in self-confidence. He played President Wintergreen in George Gershwin's classic political satire *Of Thee I Sing*, a glorious musical lampoon of the American political system. Of course Henry's singing voice left a little to be desired, but that certainly didn't dampen his ardour.

And anyway, if singing wasn't really his style, Henry found that his stage career was benefiting

from another side of his talent, that indispensable attribute of many great performers: dancing. "I think dancing is the second greatest physical action a human being can do," he says today. "I never took formal lessons. I guess I have a lot of style but not the technique. I taught myself the Russian *kazatzky* [that energetic dance in which squatting dancers kick out one leg after another, all the time keeping down on their haunches], and I went to see the film version of *West Side Story* thirteen times. I would stage one-man versions of it, taking over the whole of the apartment when my parents were out."

When his parents, it must be noted, were out. Poor Harry and Ilse Winkler — try as they might, there seemed no way they could deter Henry from his chosen path. After all, his father had devoted a good part of his life to creating a successful international lumber business and had fought against all odds to keep it going even after the traumatic flight from Germany. Surely their only son would follow in his footsteps. But as the years passed and Henry's total commitment to the theatre became absolutely undeniable, their resolve began to crumble. Today, friends say that Ilse Winkler is her son's best press agent, but not so long ago it was all an uphill struggle. Maybe that same courage and determination that helped Henry Winkler keep his business at the top despite fearful problems is the very quality that has brought his son, in a very different sphere, to the peak of his

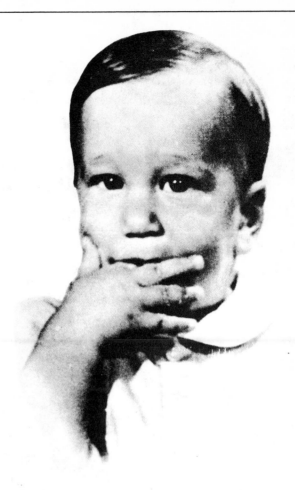

profession. As they watched him on stage, however reluctantly, Mr and Mrs Winkler had to admit that, while Henry would of course give up all this nonsense once college was over, he did have something.

And if Henry had something, then it was his life's work to improve on it, to hone it to perfection, to extend his range, his talent and his overall acting ability. Once settled at Emerson College the roles began to flow. Drama classes at McBurney had given Henry a taste for the delights of the stage. Now Emerson College, once again hardly the scene of any great intellectual achievements by our star, provided the perfect backdrop for him to pursue his acting. He carried a spear in Shakespeare's *Coriolanus*, he joined a children's theatre group that played local high schools, he played in *The Fantasticks*, his dancing won him a star role in *Finian's Rainbow* . . . the parts just kept on coming. Of course his father was still hanging on to his optimistic belief that Henry's passion for acting was in fact only infatuation. Halfway through his four years at Emerson Henry was dispatched to the West Tag lumber mill in Weidenbruck, Germany. It was the last thing Henry wanted. For a start it deprived him of his first real love, his girl-friend Suzie, but to add insult to injury, it cut him off from that other love — the stage. As he sawed up veneered wood and sang love songs to Suzie, inaudible above the sawmill's screams and whines, Henry dreamt only of the

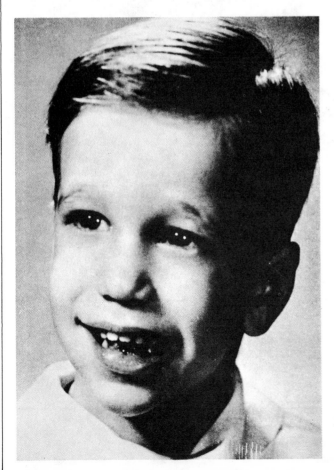

moment when he could get home again. If Harry Winkler had thought he could blunt his son's appetite for the stage he couldn't have been further from the truth. If the laborious, boring work in Germany had any effect on Henry, it was simply to intensify his dedication to the career in which he just knew he would do well.

Back in Boston it was all action once more. His affair had collapsed — Suzie was dating elsewhere — but his acting career had burgeoned. Lead roles in heavyweight plays like *Donner* and Ibsen's *Peer Gynt* took him to a new, and vitally important stage of his acting life. When *Donner* was performed by Emerson College at the annual Yale Undergraduate Dramatic School Festival, Henry suddenly realised that maybe a few years with a graduate school would develop his acting even further. He'd been wondering what to do when his years at Emerson were over, and this seemed the ideal course. After all, the lists of unemployed actors were enormous. If he was set on entering that demanding and sometimes disastrous profession, then the least a sensible guy could do was get all the advantages he could put together. He worked up a piece from both his most recent performances and set off to audition for New York and Yale University graduate schools. To his delight they both asked him to enroll in their drama courses. Prestigious Yale, with its Ivy League image, its years of scholarship, of tradition, and of great social as well as professional prospects, won his approval. "I threw open the windows of my apartment and yelled out to all of Boston, 'I'm accepted at Yale!' "

There were twenty-four people in Henry's drama class at Yale, and Henry's constant fear was that he wouldn't make it through to the end of the course. Rivalry was intense as the young actors fought for recognition and started off towards the hoped-for successes their career demanded. Soon Henry had an image: "I want instant international recognition" Winkler was how some of his classmates saw him. Some joke! But in a way, Henry couldn't deny that their jibe rang true. Anyway, why not. Acting is not a particularly self-effacing profession. Standing up there on stage in front of hundreds of people doesn't call for the more retiring of human qualities. If Henry wanted to be a success, then sure, instant international recognition would do just fine.

Graduate school at Yale was filled with opportunities to indulge those very fantasies. Visiting teachers included acting guests like Stacy Keach, Anthony Quayle, Paul Newman and Robert Redford. A cast list to whet the appetite of any aspirant star. When Henry left Emerson he was named Most Outstanding Performer, but at Yale he was in there alongside plenty of outstanding performers, all of whom had graduated from their various colleges equally respected and loaded with honours. It was at Yale that Henry learnt more and more of the finer points of his chosen art. Carmen de Lavallade, who taught Henry at Yale, remembers

If only dreams came true. It's wedding bells for Potsie and Joanie as the rest of the guys look on.

his progress there. "He wasn't always too secure, though his general cockiness kept him going, come what may. Henry didn't have much faith in himself. I was constantly trying to encourage him because people need that when they're performing. He was a perfectionist, at least I thought so, in his work and in my classes. He came to them regularly and he worked very hard."

Henry graduated from Yale in 1970 with a huge list of stage credits behind him. He split his time, like any other drama student, between major productions and 'workshop'. In the whole time he was at Yale, from 1967 to 1970, Henry appeared in about 50 plays, more than any of his contemporaries. There were classic productions of Gogol, Durenmatt, Eugene O'Neill and of course Shakespeare. And then there were workshop shows, improvisations, revue and cabaret. Henry's years at Yale coincided with the most intense period of student unrest, anti-war fervour and national discontent that America had ever experienced. Henry was too aware and sensitive to be untouched by the social and political ferment in which he was living. He and some classmates put together a radical political cabaret called *The American Pig*. The no-holds-barred analysis of the contemporary scene packed out the auditorium night after night. It was a definite underground hit. But when some of the stars wanted to move the show to New York, Henry dutifully dedicated himself to the continuation of his studies.

While he worked, learnt and performed his way through Yale, Henry's social life never let up. True to the era, Henry shared in a communal existence with six other people in a lovely house on the beach at New Haven, the town that plays host to

Yale University. "Those were two of the best years I've ever had in a living situation," he recalls. "It was a very civilized way to live, very much like a family. We just had the greatest of times, playing together and working together." His love-life didn't diminish either. With a true love of opposites, dark, New York born Henry Winkler fell for the first of what proved to be a series of sweet, blonde Southern belles.

Meanwhile the years of learning were drawing to a close. There was no longer any problem of what to do after college: Henry's mind was long since made up. The problem now was simply where to do it. He auditioned for fourteen American repertory companies in a performance in Chicago. Ten of them offered the young professional a job. But his mind had been half made up before he had even left for the audition. Robert Brustein, the head of Yale's graduate school, had already told Henry there was a place for him in Yale's top drawer professional Repertory Company if he chose to take it up. With ten other offers in his pocket, Henry made up his mind. If Yale had asked, then Yale should receive. He joined the professional company, the envied toast of his class.

Now, at last, the years of training were over. For $175 a week Henry Winkler was a genuine, professional actor. Once again, the future lay gloriously open. The awards, the honours, the praise of Emerson and Yale were great background, but how would the paying customers like the young hopeful? A Master of Fine Arts, a paid up card-carrying member of Actor's Equity, Henry Winkler was on his way. The question was very simple: where would it lead him. Henry naturally had just one answer: to the top, to the very top.

CHAPTER 3
I'M ONLY MAKING IT

"I had no guarantee for work. I came out to Hollywood with a thousand dollars and hope. Eight days after I arrived I cried myself to sleep."

They're a dime a dozen, the young hopefuls who plunge into the acting profession. And there's not one of them who doesn't reckon themselves worth a million dollars. Henry Winkler, for instance. Just signed up with the Yale Repertory Company in 1970, working for his first regular salary of $175 a week, all crazy-keen on success and raring to go.

Naturally, for the still less than totally self-confident Henry, there was plenty of that good old Jewish *angst* mixed in with the ego that is the vital part of anyone who's prepared to get up on stage and play with the world's emotions. "It was a very ambivalent time for me, because here I am getting paid and I'm saying 'Am I worth it? Do I have the talent to actually be paid for what I want to do?' All that stuff. So that coloured my performances quite a lot. Yet some of the best reviews I ever got were during that first summer."

Ask any theatre person — they'll tell you that of all the stage's varied forms, the weekly Repertory Company is undoubtedly its most gruelling. The proving ground for many an embryo star, Repertory, with its basic formula of 'new day — new play' has carved out some of the finest talents in acting. It has also taken its toll of many young professionals who simply couldn't make the grade. It's tough, demanding and, for Henry Winkler, totally delightful.

That first summer acting for Yale was jam-packed with parts, and with the sort of praises that make the performing even sweeter. Henry played in works by such diverse authors as Philip Roth, Gustave Flaubert, Isaac Basshevis Singer, Dashiell Hammett and Ovid. A weird and wonderfully assorted bunch! and all grist to the young actor's professional mill. Then, with his part in Cyril Tourneur's classic *Revenger's Tragedy*, Henry first came to the attention of that West Coast mecca of stardom, Hollywood. Cliff Robertson had seen Henry performing in an earlier show that year, "I'll remember you," he'd promised. That, reasoned Henry, was what he told all the boys. Yet a few months later, there was a long-distance call for Henry as he stepped off stage. Sure enough, it *was* Cliff Robertson. "Get on the plane to the coast," he told Henry, "I have a good part for you in my next film."

The movies! Fame, fortune . . . the whole glorious fantasy that Henry had grown up watching in the theatre, in musicals and on the screen. So Henry, with hardly a moment's pause, did what possibly no other young actor in his position would have done: he turned the offer down! There were, of course, some excellent and sensible reasons, but it just shows Henry's maturity as he managed to avoid a lightning decision in favour of moving further and further towards the perfection he felt his acting demanded. After all, he reckoned quite logically, where one offer comes, can another be so far behind? Not only that, but his part in *The Revenger's Tragedy* (he played a sixteen-year-old rapist and got his only bad review, "They said I had a New York accent") was still running, and there was no understudy. Robert Brustein, the director, generously offered to let Henry go, even at such short notice, but Henry wanted to stay. If those offers did start flowing in, then the more prepared he was, the better.

The Gods, as ever, were up to their tricks. If there had been a measure of pride in Henry's rejection of a Hollywood offer, so sure was he that others were just sitting there in the pipeline, then there was a fall in the offing. In summer 1971 he quit Yale Repertory Company. He'd been there a year, a very successful year, and he wanted a

change. He went to New York and auditioned successfully for a role in *Moonchildren*, a play Washington's Arena Theatre were putting on. Then, after three weeks of rehearsal, came the thunderbolt. On the last night of rehearsals, at the traditional pre-show party, the director called Henry to one side. "Henry," he said, "for whatever reason, I have replaced you in the cast." As Henry put it later, "My brain immediately turned into cream cheese." And then some. There he was, Henry Winkler, superstar in the making, Mr "I want immediate international recognition" himself, fired!

Suddenly, the golden boy found himself out in the cold. He had quit Yale, been tossed out of Washington. There was only one place to go: New York City, the voracious Big Apple itself. He moved into Greenwich Village, that haven for the weird and the wonderful, and started eking out what little he'd saved from his career to date. Not surprisingly, it wasn't much. One thing was imperative: he had to find work, any work, as soon as possible. Like a million other actors before him, Henry's first job, to fill in while he was, in actor's parlance "resting", was nothing to do with the stage. He worked days in a travel agency. Every morning, on the way to work, he checked out the upcoming auditions. When they came up, he turned up. But it seemed that nobody wanted to know. All the praise in the world seemed pretty

irrelevant now. Back he would trudge, dejected and deflated, to his desk at the travel bureau.

It took six weeks of soul-destroying grind before Henry broke free of the airline bookings and the luxury hotel reservations. "I started doing commercials because I couldn't get arrested elsewhere," he says today. "I did thirty commercials. I got real good at getting them. In fact I got to the point where I could get two a day, all Class A television commercials. That was great because it allowed me to do plays at night for free." The story was a little more complex than that, at the time. His entry into the lucrative, if scarcely artistic, world of the commercial came less through his immediate acting talent than through his taste, unchanged, for those cute Southern belles. Another brief entanglement — Henry, alas, tended to fancy them more than they did him — led to an introduction to an agent, Joan Scott, who is Henry's agent to this day. But even Joan, try as she might, was having a tough time finding Henry roles. Until someone suggested TV commercials. Off ran Henry to Grey Advertising, who were casting a spot for Talon Zippers. He auditioned and won the part. In fact the Talon ad was never televised, but for Henry it was the start of a good career in commercials.

The products that Henry, in one role or another, happily endorsed were many and varied. He ate thirty-five pizzas for one product — they had to get it just right — and smiled for half an hour straight in a toothpaste ad. He even told the world how deadly marijuana was in one anti-dope spot. And there were many, many more. Each of them "starring" Henry Winkler. Trouble was that was about all the starring he was doing. As 1971 became 1972 and his commercial career boomed, Henry could have been forgiven for thinking here, if nothing else, was security. But Henry was hardly about to dedicate himself to the fickle fate of what was, in all honesty, nothing more than male modelling with movements. Going through his paces to boost Schick Razor Blades or the A&P grocery chain was hardly the kind of career Henry had in mind when he went through the long years of training for his performing life. Money, inevitably, was not enough. As any student of Henry's career will have realised by now, what our hero needed was another good break. And as those same students will also appreciate, the break duly arrived.

He was working with a revue called *Off The Wall* — they wrote all their own material and worked regularly for some months — when one of his acting partners in the show mentioned a new movie to him. It was called *The Lords of Flatbush* and featured the rough and tumble life of the three guys who made up The Lords: a New York greaser gang straight out of the fifties. Henry called up his agent and had her arrange an audition. Off he went and when the producer offered him a role, he couldn't wait to say yes. Henry Winkler, smiling star of the toothpaste commercials, was a thing of the past. Now he was reborn, for the moment

anyway, as Butchy Weinstein, all leather jacket and ducktail haircut, motorcycle boots and tight jeans. He walked with a swagger and the kids in the neighbourhood worshipped him. Butchy was the third, supporting member of a gang that starred two other names that the world would be watching very shortly. There was Stanley — played by Sylvester *Rocky* Stallone — and Chico — played by Perry King of *Mandingo* and *Lipstick* fame. Henry brought a three-dimensional quality to the artistic loner who balanced his intellectual pretentions against the hard street life of The Lords.

The movie was no great hit, though it soon gained what the buffs call 'cult status'. *Playboy* Magazine gave it a fine review, and called it "realistically photographed and explosively funny, an honest and downbeat recollection of what it was like to be growing up in the fifties". All good stuff but the great nostalgia boom that, apart from Henry's own personality, has undoubtedly helped *Happy Days* to score such a knockout success, was still holding off. No matter, even if the theatres weren't as jam-packed as Henry might have desired, it was incredibly good experience. And now other work was coming in. Henry was given his Broadway debut in *42 Seconds From Broadway*. He was the lead, but the play flopped disastrously and lasted only barely longer than its title. It came off after one night. Henry was undaunted. He rebounded as if the flop had never happened and went off to Connecticut for a role in *Incident At Vichy*.

Then another movie role was offered. *Crazy Joe* was another of those pulp-Mafia films, cashing in on the box office bonanza that came to the makers of *The Godfather*. Loosely based on New York's

Hail, Hail, the gang's all here (left to right) Ralph Malph, you know who, Potsie Weber and Richie Cunningham.

mobster Crazy Joe Gallo, who was gunned down by gangland assassins, the movie starred Peter Boyle, Paula Prentiss and Eli Wallach. Henry was Mannie: "Crazy Joe's most solid supporter, a soldier in the gang wars who fought with Joe and didn't desert him when he was in prison." *Crazy Joe* was no great movie and it didn't exactly break any box office records. Henry was almost unrecognisable in his seedy role. A suit and tie, even a moustache — it was a far cry from the roles he had been playing of late. Still, financial failure or not, Henry knew *Crazy Joe* for what it was as far as he was concerned. "It was an important film. It placed me in a different league because of the stars who were in it. Even if I was always in the shadow of these people — and rightly so — the movie projected me in an entirely different light than *The Lords* did."

It was while he was still basking in this new light that Henry, bolstered up by his agent, made a new and vital decision. The East Coast, even New York

City had its limitations. It was time for Henry to make a move geographically which might, if luck and his talent were with him, turn into a move upwards and onwards in a career which, in all fairness, had yet to catch alight. "I kept thinking, what are they going to want with a short Jewish kid in Hollywood?" says Henry, but in September 1973, that was just where he was headed. For a while it was touch and go. "Every day for two weeks my agent would say 'It's time for you to go' and I'd say 'No'," but eventually Henry gave in. What actually changed his mind was the discovery that his co-star and friend from *The Lords*, Perry King, had also decided it was time to make the big move. They flew out together. Two hopefuls with no job, no address, no friends to greet them. Just a thousand dollars in his pocket and plenty of optimism in his heart.

If the acting profession contains its thousands of hopefuls, then its Hollywood department must contain millions. The myths of instant recognition,

of overnight stardom, of "discovery" are too strong in America's consciousness to leave the field open to the professionals alone. For every Henry Winkler, with years of training, of experience, of even a couple of film appearances not to mention hundreds of stage roles, there are plenty of no-talent optimists, trekking into the showbiz mecca, desperate to succeed. The competition for success is frightening. And Henry admits that after a week sleeping on a sofa, he was as frightened as the next guy.

"I had no guarantee for work, nothing. I came out here with a thousand dollars and hope. Eight days after I got out here," he recalls, "I cried myself to sleep. I was that scared and frustrated." His agent had persuaded him to make the trip, now he was told, "It's going to be very hard to sell you out here." "I figured it was a three thousand mile, thousand dollar mistake someone had made with my life."

But the depression didn't last. It couldn't — not

if Henry was going to make something of his chances in Hollywood. The first, and most sensible thing he did was move out of his temporary apartment and find a bed of his own instead of someone else's sofa. He spent a short time sharing a place, then moved to the Sunset Marquis Hotel, a home from home for out of town actors. If any clue was needed as to how Henry had got himself together, it came the day his car, the precious wheels anyone had to have in Los Angeles where no one ever walks, was totalled in a smash. Two weeks before Henry might have packed his bags and quit. Now he just laughed.

There were other, more concrete reasons than his apartment in the hotel. For someone with as little patience as Henry admits to having, the long slog that is supposed to go before a Hollywood career was the one thing he couldn't and wouldn't face. And in October, just a couple of weeks after he'd arrived, Henry's agent told him to line up for an audition for one of America's favourite comedy

shows: *The Mary Tyler Moore Show*. This was more like it. Henry auditioned and won a small part. It was a whole week's work. When the show was aired the MTM organisation took another look at Henry and realised that they had a useful property on their hands. After that first week's work, Henry was asked back to put in time on other shows organised by Mary Tyler Moore and her husband Grant Tinkler. There was *The Bob Newhart Show*, the pilot for *The Paul Sand Show* and more.

Then, as Henry settled into a regular round of television bit-parts, his agent called again. She'd arranged an interview for him at the Paramount Studios. "It's just to meet them. They're casting a pilot for a series called *Happy Days* and they're looking for a real tough guy greaser type. You're all wrong, but go in and see them."

CHAPTER 4
ENTER THE FONZ

*"Every actor has played this type of guy.
I knew there had to be another
side to him…"*

The lobby at Paramount Studios was packed. To Henry's anxious eyes it looked like wall to wall superstars, every one dressed to kill in one or another version of the fifties greaser role. When he'd come in through the studio gates and the guard had known his name, he'd wondered if maybe this was his big day. Now, surrounded by what looked like a hundred guys just made for the part, he slumped. "The guy ahead of me had gone in with his hair greased and in a DA. That guy was Mickey Dolenz of the Monkees. An established star was going in there and they didn't even know me. What chance did I have? I was thinking: 'I'm out of the running. I don't even know why I'm here and I'm scared.' Then I walked in and I said, 'I really don't think I'm the guy you're looking for.' "

As ever, the famous Winkler self-criticism was coming to the fore just when it wasn't needed. Henry was shutting down his attack before it had even been put to a test. Tom Milkis, of Miller-Milkis — the producers of *Happy Days* — wasn't fooled so easily. Along with the panel of ABC-TV executives, producers, directors, casting people and so on, Milkis handed Henry the half dozen lines that made up the audition for a small part in their upcoming show: Arthur Fonzarelli, the street-wise dropout who adds a little spice to the Cunningham family and to Jefferson High School's all-American image.

October 30th, the day after the audition and Henry's birthday. The phone rang with a birthday gift that Henry might have dreamt of but had already tossed aside. ABC wanted him to come back for another reading. In fact, it was made pleasantly clear that unless he totally blew up on this second time around, Henry Winkler was dead set to join the *Happy Days* outfit. Shaking with terror, Henry was ushered straight into the producers' room at Paramount Pictures. This time he had to convince Barry Diller, ABC-TV's Director of Programming. It was the same scene as last time and as 'Fonzie' reached his last line, "and don't ever do that again", Henry swept majestically out of the room, slamming the door behind him. Then he shook with fear once more until Tom Miller came out and said how good the reading was, and that they'd be in touch. "The next thing that happened was an hour and a half long telephone conversation with Tom Miller from my room at the Sunset Marquis. They wanted me for Fonzie!"

So there he was, Henry Winkler, twenty-eight year old actor, nine years in training and his whole life dedicated to pursuing the career he *knew* would be right for his particular talents. Now, just a few scant weeks after coming to Hollywood, he was the proud possessor of that coveted prize — a role in a series. You could almost call it an over-night success. Almost that is, until you started totting up all the years of training, of discipline, of gradually perfecting his acting abilities. Just like all those who are branded instant stars, the instant bit is only in the public's eyes. For the actor himself, the night has sometimes been very long indeed.

And the Fonz himself wasn't just flying up there at the top of the ratings as soon as the show was aired. For a start Henry wanted to be so sure of his position as the duck-tailed hoodlum that he told Tom Miller just what he was and was not prepared to do. *Before* he'd even accepted the offer of the role. "I don't know where I got the courage. I said I would like to play the character, but I would only do it if they allowed me the freedom to play him multi-dimensional." It says a good deal both for Henry's sense of himself and Tom Miller's realisation that here was a sincere and talented actor, not some posing egocentric, that he went along with Henry's demands. He accepted Henry's position, and the rules that Henry laid down in that first tentative telephone call have survived until today — and, no doubt, have helped enormously in making both the role of Fonzie and the style of *Happy Days* as a whole so extraordinarily successful.

"Every actor has always played this kind of a tough guy," said Henry, "there's *got* to be another side to him. Furthermore," he laid down, "I will not have a cigarette pack in my shirt sleeve, I will not wear a belt, I will not chew gum, I will never comb my hair . . ." Rules that can be seen in action on every episode of *Happy Days* right up till now.

If Henry had stated his position on his new character, then he soon learnt that rule making was a two-way process. There probably doesn't exist in the world so delicately balanced a medium as American network television. The obsessive desire to avoid bruising *any* sensibilities — from the sponsor, to the public at large (not to mention all those active minority groups whose lobbies can decimate movies, television, advertising and pretty much everything else) to the network executives themselves — means that a television show today has to ride an incredibly thin line between all those different opinions. The net result, as anyone can see from a million bland Stateside products, is a stream of shows that spend so much time saying nothing to offend that they end up, surprise, surprise, saying nothing!

It says a good deal for Henry, not forgetting the producers who chose him for the part, that many of ABC's initial rulings on The Fonz were side-stepped or ignored or just subtly altered. Take the case of that Fonzarelli trademark — his leather jacket. Now ABC, in their wisdom, had decreed that no way would any character on their show be seen in leather. Leather was degenerate, dirty and equated in the family mind with violence, perversion and crime. Leather, and its partner, grease (in the hair, rather than under the Fonz's mechanic's fingernails) meant a criminal mentality, OK. Except that Henry *didn't* think it was OK. Not at all. ABC had issued him a tan cloth wind-breaker (a *wind*breaker, for heaven's sake!) but he really couldn't get Fonzie together with that. One week, early in the series, he just put on a leather jacket, lovingly treasured and battered by years of wear. Nobody noticed, or if they did nobody commented, and the jacket, as Fonzie fans are well aware, stayed. The same went for Fonzie's foot-wear. The costume department had given Henry a pair of loafers. Once again Henry didn't want to know. He persuaded the producers that what his role demanded was the kind of tough motorcycle boots — called engineer boots in the States — that he'd worn as Butchy Weinstein in *The Lords of Flatbush*. Indeed, he told Tom Miller, they still happened to be around in New York. Miller agreed and on his next trip to New York, Henry picked

Off the set Henry Winkler dresses to please himself. And that goes for his role as a Fonzie too.

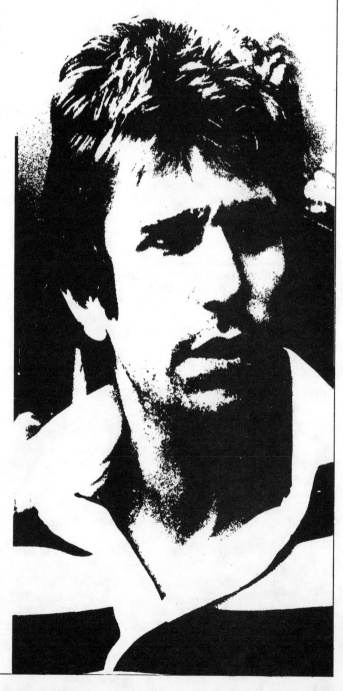

Henry the 'Hero' — on set in New York

up the boots. They too became part of the Fonzie personality.

Top of the bill, of course, came Fonzie's crowning glory — his hair. If leather jackets and heavy boots were theoretically out, then the grease-slicked ducktail hairstyle that was totally obligatory for every fifties punk just had those ABC executives cringing. This was corruption rampant — it just could *not* happen. And even today, with Fonzie topping world-wide ratings, that's one ruling Henry still can't buck. Yet, and you may well ask, why is it that when Henry plays The Fonz, it does *seem* that he's laced his dark locks with around half a tub of Brylcreem? Very simple, though the logic behind what ABC decided to do is less obvious: first Henry's hair is wetted and combed and sprayed and styled into the correct ducktail shape. That takes about thirty minutes to dry then the whole process is repeated. The finished product can be checked any time you tune in to a segment of *Happy Days*. Yes, it does look as if Henry has grease on his hair; no, he definitely doesn't.

Finally, there's the combing of those same sculpted strands. Henry, right from the start of his involvement with the show, refused point-blank to go through that cliche-ridden ritual of combing his

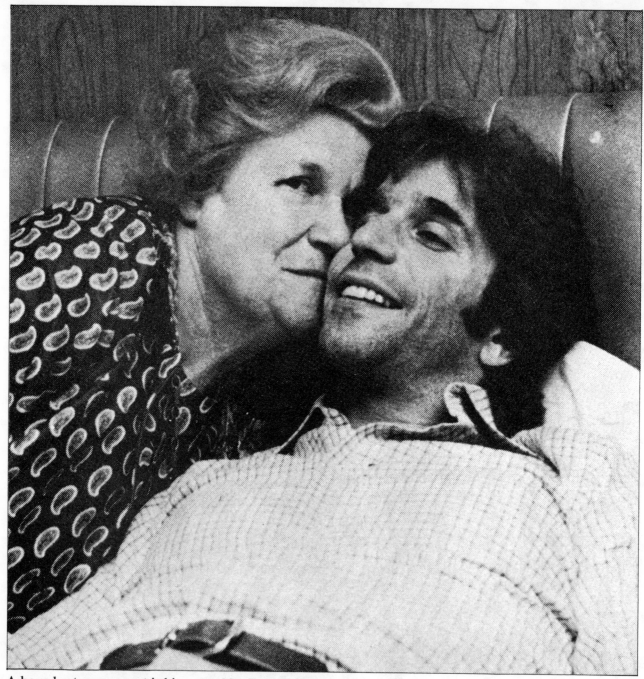

A boys best press agent is his mom. Mrs Ilse Winkler gives her favourite boy a hug.

hair lovingly and at length. Inevitably, as they put together the pilot show that was aimed at selling the whole series both to the public and to the network on a permanent basis, one of the directors demanded that, like it or not, Henry should comb his hair. "The director wanted it, but I was afraid if I did it once I'd be stuck with it forever. Necessity became the mother of my invention. I walked to the mirror, pulled out my comb and brought it up to my hair. Then, as I recognised that my hair was perfect, I said 'he-e-e-ey' with satisfaction, put the comb away and walked out."

It wasn't just his hair that was perfect. Anyone who's seen the show and checked out that great credits sequence where Fonzie makes that very

play with his comb will realise that here was real acting style and ability. Talk about a star is born! In that one minutely judged gesture, Henry brought the Fonz to glorious life. The King of Cool was born and soon the world's television audiences would be his happy subjects.

Of course the Arthur Fonzarelli character didn't start off his life in *Happy Days* with quite the starring role he has today. When that first pilot was put together, Fonzie rated seventh in importance on the show. He had three scenes and only in one of them did he actually speak a meagre eight lines. The "he-e-e-ey" and "whoa" sounds that now have half the western world trying to imitate them were about all the script Henry was given

Nobody loves them, everyone hates them and Henry Winkler's worms don't appeal to Sally Field.

back in that early show. In those first episodes, Fonzie had a much less central role. He was a sex symbol for the girls — he knew his way, as he revealed in the pilot, around such intricacies as a bra-strap and had to explain it all to an incredulous, but keen, Potsie and Richie. He was a dropout and got to ride a meaty motorcycle. He was "cool" and as such someone for the three Jefferson High School boys to emulate and look up to. Though make no mistake — the Fonz needs those well-intentioned nerds as much as they need him. It's the relationship between Fonzie and in particular Richie Cunningham that makes for so much of the show's long-running impact.

As anyone who watched the early *Happy Days*

will remember, it was in fact Richie Cunningham, played by veteran actor — in credits if not in years — Ron Howard, who was set up as the actual lead character. And today, with Fonzie firmly established at the top of the *Happy Days* tree, Richie is the only person who can hope to rival his appeal. Robert Hoffman, the show's dialogue coach, underlines this basic and highly important relationship. "The key is, the Fonz is untouchable. You just can't touch the Fonz. Only Richie can, and he'll never make the overture. If Potsie ever touched the Fonz, we'd be dead." Henry Winkler can never say strongly enough how much he owes to Ronnie Howard. "I haven't done it all myself," he points out today. "I could not do it without

‘Fearless Fonzarelli’: its all systems go for the Evel Kenivel of Arnold’s Drive-In.

Ron Howard, there's no way I could have done it without him."

Indeed, when Tom Miller wanted a second opinion on casting Henry as the Fonz, it was Ron to whom he turned. "They wanted to bring in a big tall guy," explains Ron, "but Tom pushed very hard to get Henry in there. Tom came up to me and said, 'What do you think of Henry?' right after the first reading. And I said 'Well, he's really great'. I mean even just sitting around the table reading the first script he was fantastic. He only had a few lines in the first show and yet Tom said, 'I don't know what it is about this guy, but he's going to be a star'."

Tom Miller, how right you were. As the first series worked its way up the vital Neilsen ratings that determine whether a show stands or falls for the American public, not to mention whether audiences abroad ever get the chance of watching the latest product from across the Atlantic, it became increasingly clear that a good proportion of the popularity Happy Days was getting came from the magnetic personality of its seventh rated character, Arthur Fonzarelli, The Fonz. For a guy

so low on the credits, Henry was pulling in an enormous bundle of fan mail. It didn't take all that much professional know-how to realise how much the fans loved this finely observed and expressively acted portrayal of a cliche fifties character who, maybe for the first time ever on the screen, wasn't cliched. Henry's obsession with detail, his determination to perfect the role, was paying off. Both for ABC and for the actor himself.

"Because we're basically about the 1950s," says Ron Howard, "I felt we would remain on the air for two and a half to three years. I thought we'd go on at mid-season and be moderately successful. I felt we would kind of hold our own our second year and then our third year that would be it. Nostalgia would be over and so would the show." Which is not, as Happy Days producers, actors and fans will be the first to tell you, quite what happened. Today, topping the ratings in America, Australia, Canada and the UK, Happy Days rates among some of the most successful television shows in the history of the medium. The Happy Days success story is a remarkable phenomenon and within it there is contained another story equally amazing: the rise of Henry Winkler, or The Fonzie Phenomenon.

CHAPTER 5
THE FONZIE PHENOMENON

*"Fonzie is spontaneous. He lives hard
and loves fast and no-one ever uses
his comb."*

What can you say about a guy who's really made it? Up there at the top with one of the most successful television series ever brought to the small screen. A guy who can pull in over one hundred million world wide viewers for thirty compelling minutes every week. Who gets more than 50,000 fan letters each week. Who has to have the kind of security operation mounted for his public appearances that would put a Presidential motorcade to shame. What, to cut all the statistics short, can you say about Henry Winkler, creator of The Fonz?

"Fonzie gets his cool through integrity," Henry has pointed out, and Henry's own new-found status as television's hottest screen personality is continually underlined by the star's own integrity. In the face of Fonzie buttons, T-shirts, posters and the whole range of merchandising that hits him on every street corner, not to mention the fans who write in, and always remembering the money that comes with this kind of success, Henry remains the same barely confident, self-effacing man he has always been.

In the first place, amidst all the zany publicity barrage, the campaigns of "Fonzie for President" and the like, the whole wonderful brouhaha that runs hand in glove with a smash hit like *Happy Days*, there's always this small, but emphatic voice coming out with the same old theme: "I am not Arthur Fonzarelli, I am Henry Winkler."

Henry is adamant on that point. And he's making a deliberate point of, as he puts it, "educating the public" to accept his point of view. "I never *knew* anyone like Fonzie when I was growing up; in fact if a Fonzie *had* shown up in my world, I would probably have feigned blindness so he'd leave me alone." You can see what Henry

means. Check those early pictures of summer camp Henry, Bar Mitzvah boy Henry, Joe College Fraternity boy Henry. The Fonz would definitely *not* be hanging around with that sort of nerd. Cool? No *way*. While the youthful Fonzie was just easing his way through life, making sure all the cards fell in the right direction, Henry Winkler was, on his own admission, the usual tortured adolescent. "Fonzie and I are as opposite as two men can be."

Difference is one thing, though Henry's love and respect for the character he plays is as sincere as his refusal to let the great public type him for ever in the same role. "It's been a national campaign on my part to emphasize that Fonzie is my fantasy. If I don't keep a perspective, if I start to believe that I am more than I am, I'm dead. I cannot start living an image. If I start to live an image I will live one day behind myself. I will never be Henry Winkler. The reality is that I've been Henry for thirty-two years and I respond best to that. I am not Fonzie, I do not want to be him. He is my job. I love to create him. But that is where the line is drawn."

Fair enough, Henry. Except the fans really don't believe that kind of tough, honest statement. After the reception he received as King of the New Orleans Mardi Gras, Henry looked out on the screaming thousands of fans and mused, "I know what it was like to be a Beatle." More recently, another less pleasant aspect of Fonziemania hit him. Not so long ago some nut was forecasting that Paul McCartney of the Beatles had been killed. The rumour swept the media — many people still wonder if Paul really is who he claims to be. This time the jokers started on Henry Winkler. Except that the joke was pretty sour. It started when Henry's sister Bea picked up the phone in her Dallas home to hear that her brother was dead. A month later Henry himself read reports in the

Australian press that he had died in a car smash. Next came the Omaha radio station that told its listeners that The Fonz was dead — of a drug overdose. At that stage the big boys weighed in. The Associated Press and United Press International contacted ABC-TV to check the bizarre rumour. Henry was alive and well, sure enough, but the sour taste lingers. "I have no idea how that started," says Henry. "I'm not interested either. If people want to think I'm dead and cause such a ruckus, I'm very flattered except that I wish it was more positive. That kind of publicity I can do without."

It's not the only drawback that comes with superstardom. "It never occurred to me that fame could be something less than a pleasure. You learn all too soon that fame is an illusion conjured by an adoring public and to be famous you must pay its price." Sad words, but impressive too. After all, Henry has hardly been up there in the superstar bracket for that long. Many infinitely more experienced stars have yet to learn that tough lesson. It shows yet again the kind of mature man that Henry Winkler is and just underlines the fact that if Henry takes a position, then the media and the public might as well take that position seriously.

Yet Henry loves the Fonz, despite all the hassles. And if anyone's starting to murmur something about crying all the way to the bank, then sure, Henry doesn't mind admitting that playing Fonzie for around a reputed $15,000 per episode, has certainly taken him out of the low-rent hotels and secondhand car marts of this world. Not that Henry was ever a poor boy, but don't let the stories of the "millionaire Winklers" fool you. "I'm no little rich kid making good," says Henry. He's worked for his success and in America, and most other places too, that means plenty of money. "I don't have to choose the $3.95 special for dinner

any more," he jokes. And it's true. For Henry these days, life comes strictly *a la carte*.

The real reason, of course, why Henry loves his role in *Happy Days* is far removed from picking up that fat pay cheque. Over and above everything else Henry Winkler is an actor. The Fonz is a role that his talents have elevated from a bit part with eight lines to an international figure whose mannerisms, vocabulary and lifestyle half the world's teenagers seem keen on copying. "My career," he stresses over and over again, "is my priority." First and foremost he is an actor. When Henry worries about being typecast he is genuinely worried. The series has brought him fame and fortune, or as he puts it, "I am acting, working hard and making a good living at it," but it is not, and as far as Henry is concerned must not write, the bottom line to his professional ambitions. He wants to star in a film, he wants to write and direct a film. Hardly exceptional ambitions for an actor, but how many members of his over-stocked and under-employed trade actually get the opportunity to put those fantasies into action. For Henry today the problem is not when, but which, not fear of rejection but the difficulties of personal selection. "All I'm interested in is becoming a better actor.

As soon as *Happy Days* ends I'm going to concentrate on films. Sure, adulation is part of why I act, but when I'm doing the work I don't think about the adulation. I think about creating the perfect character in the sky. About creating the perfect energy. What an artist can do with his paintbrush and his imagination and his eyes, I can do. My whole body is the paintbrush."

Some ideal — though one that Henry Winkler is dead set on making a reality. What, on the other hand, would the King of Cool make of that kind of talk. Maybe, believe it or not, more than you might think. Because there's a side to dropout Fonzie that Henry, and many of his older fans, have noticed. Hoodlum-type he may be, but there's a whole lot more to The Fonz than a ducktail cut and a leather jacket. And we don't mean a whole drive-in full of adoring girls either. He's been set up time and time again as an example to kids all over the place. Not as a dropout, but as a guy with integrity, with loyalty, courage and a whole lot more of what Mr Cunningham might well call "sterling qualities". Henry says, "Fonzie isn't a bad image. Nobody's dropped out of school because of him. And whenever I talk to kids, I tell them to stay in school." Anyway, Fonzie's dropout role is

the least important aspect of the image that Henry puts over on the *Happy Days* set. The reason fifty-odd thousand fans put adoring pen to paper every week isn't because Fonzie cut school, it's because he's so totally cool, so efficient with his own life and everyone else's. Henry's called him "a big brother" to the rest of the Jefferson High gang. No offense, Arthur, but the guy sometimes acts like the "Dear Marge" of the grease pit. Henry quite unashamedly is as big a fan of the character he's brought to life as are the public who turn to *Happy Days* every week. "Fonzie is spontaneous. He lives hard and loves fast and no one ever uses his comb. That may sound like a lot of words but it really means something. You don't mess around with the Fonz and he doesn't mess around with you, either. If you're straight with him, he'll be straight back."

The "cool" that epitomises Fonzie is very much the product of Henry's own concept of that hard to define characteristic. "When I began creating the character, I started with the concept of cool. I decided that 'cool' comes from the centre, the core of a person. It comes from integrity. Fonzie's vulnerability, his loyalty are part of his cool and I try to let that peek through the coat of leather from time to time. Another element in his cool is his sense of morality. He stands on his own two feet; he doesn't take anything from anybody. I think all these elements make Fonzie work for the audience." And though he'd be the last to say it, maybe if integrity is the source of cool, then Henry himself isn't so different from his screen role after all. Fonzie wouldn't be the guy he is if Henry hadn't asserted *his* integrity, *his* cool right from the moment that he started to make the part his own.

So there we have it. More than a few of the many facets of the Fonzie Phenomenon. Fans all over the world know and love the character. What makes Fonzie tick for each individual is bound to be something special and different, as special and different as the man himself. But one thing remains, whatever he may say, wherever he progresses, Henry Winkler may not be the Fonz, but there certainly wouldn't be any Fonzie without him.

CHAPTER 6
BEYOND THE FONZ

"I'm having a good time. I'm doing what I love to do. But one day it could all go away, just like that."

So here he is: Henry Winkler, thirty-two years old, topping the TV ratings in half the western world, adored by millions, an actor at the top of his profession who stars in the hottest all-family series on the small screen. The man who was once teasingly nicknamed "I want instant international recognition" has now taken the joke and tossed it back in his detractors' faces. Maybe the recognition wasn't that instant — overnight success has a knack of taking a few years before the glorious dawn finally breaks — but it sure is international. Which leaves only a couple of questions: how does Henry himself see his phenomenal status, and what does he intend to do with it next?

It's all a long way from those sheltered, privileged days as a nice middle class youngster from the Upper West Side. "Right now," says Henry, "I'm trying to evaluate exactly what I've got. What does this all mean. What kind of life is this? Is this viable, is it productive, is it important? I don't know. I have a feeling that I will eventually walk away from this and do something else, because I enjoy very much being good at what I do. I do not want to be small potatoes."

Small potatoes? Anyone who has seen Henry Winkler act, on the *Happy Days* set or anywhere else for that matter, knows that he is destined to become a major actor. Of course his role as Fonzie has already brought him that kind of plaudit, but the future for a man like Henry, just thirty-two but very clear about where he's going, is infinitely wide — the possibilities are endless. To date, Henry has spent more time sifting through numerous movie and TV offers than he has on moving into new realms of acting. Movie houses in America and the rest of the countries that feature *Happy Days* are queuing up to re-run those few films Henry has

already made. *The Lords of Flatbush* has become more than just the cult show it once was, and the subsequent superstardom of both Henry and his co-star Sly Stallone have the fans delirious with pleasure. Even *Crazy Joe*, the Mafia exploitation picture, has been dragged out of the mothballs for new showings — with the former bit player's name well above the title these days. Henry has already turned down many offers to develop both his *Lords* . . . and his Fonzie roles. "I've already been offered and turned down the starring role in four series. *The Lords of Flatbush*, two different Fonzie spinoffs and a *Serpico* [the series starring David Burney, itself a spinoff from the real-life cop drama that starred Al Pacino, one of Henry Winkler's favourite actors]. I turned them down for the same reason I originally accepted the role Fonzie in *Happy Days* — because I like challenge. I need something *new*."

One brand new post-Fonzie role that Henry has played is the rebellious college radical 'Bob Klein' in the 1975 made-for-TV movie *Katherine*. Starring Art *The Late Show* Carney and Sissy *Three Women* Spacek as well as Henry, *Katherine* reads like a spinoff from Patty Hearst's adventures with the super-radical Symbionese Liberation Army. Katherine, played by Sissy Spacek, is the revolutionary bomb-tossing heroine. Bob, played by Henry, is her boyfriend. "To view Bob," said reviewer Thom Montgomery, "is to view the modern Fonzie. The subtle differences are there and Winkler does an astonishing job in bringing them forth. Winkler brings out the differences and manages nonetheless to bring out the striking similarities. As an actor it is as though Winkler (as Bob) were searching for Fonzie. And, as we know, he found him. It is a remarkable accomplishment."

Remarkable accomplishment apart, the Fonz is

still Henry's main role, though his kind of mass appeal has brought him guest spots on many of America's most popular shows, such as the *Dinah Shore Show*, the *Mike Douglas Show* and of course Johnny Carson's world famous *Tonight Show*. He's also put in the odd appearance as Fonzie on another top-rated ABC-TV show *Laverne and Shirley* — played by Penny Marshall and Cindy Williams — which itself was a spinoff from *Happy Days*. Indeed, most of the *Happy Days* gang have checked in to Laverne and Shirley's wacky show by now.

"The next frontier for me is the big screen," says Henry. "I want to make films. In television you must always understate yourself . . . but in film, the distance between your imagination and its realisation is minimal. Because you are allowed to limit your audience in film, you are able to represent life truthfully." What with bigger budgets, less of television's savage deadliness — shooting a weekly show is almost unbelievably gruelling — and a generally more flexible mode of production, Henry is sure that it is in the other side of Hollywood, the movie studios rather than the television ones, that his future lies. "I think more important work gets done on film and I'd like to be part of it." In the mean time, Henry awaits the perfect role, with a couple of scripts in the making right now.

Fonzie fans will be more than just interested to see Henry in *Heroes*, the first of two movies he's decided to let himself work on. The plot centres on an ex-Vietnam War veteran who has returned to the States and finds that life is desperately hard to readjust to. It's a poignant, perceptive story, and one that is all too true in modern America. His second venture *Georgeous George* is another slice of life, based around the great US wrestler whose flamboyant showcasing of his own talents has made him the greatest moneyspinner in Stateside grappling. One more film, according to recent Hollywood reports, may have appealed to Henry. Not surprisingly, since Henry is still very much involved with the Orthodox Judaism of his youth and family, he is looking very seriously at a script that would have him playing an immigrant Hasidic (ultra-Orthodox) rabbi, who comes to San Francisco to establish a training school for rabbis. Religion, indeed, is still central to much of Henry's life and he persists in many of his early beliefs. For instance, like any truly orthodox Jew, he will never write down the Lord's name in full. Instead, he prefers the spelling "G–d".

It's with a religious image that he defines his own incredible stardom as well. He's said that his fame has almost made him feel like God, though he's the first to qualify the statement. After all, Henry's been compared to the Beatles in terms of massive world-wide popularity, and America still hasn't completely absolved John Lennon for his remark about the group and Jesus. "I mean," says Henry in a recent *Playboy* Magazine interview, "in the moral, not the religious concept of God. It's

just that when you are at the pinnacle of power, you feel like a great conqueror, like a hero, like the best gladiator. You are pumped up with energy, it's incredible. I'm made to think about myself all the time. Every time I turn around I see myself."

But if Henry appreciates his enormous success and the power that success brought with it, then it is another mark of his maturity that he sees that he is still the same man, despite the images — both physical and metaphorical — that are thrust upon him. To put it quite simply, he's more than well aware of the transience of fame. "I'm having a good time. I'm doing what I love to do and apparently at this moment in my life, I'm doing it pretty well. One day it could all go away. Just like that." In the meantime, however, he's not ashamed to enjoy what stardom has brought him. And to accept the bad along with the good. "I know I've said that today I'm called a star, that today I'm a celebrity, that today I receive generous offers. It's all true but please note that I qualify each statement with the word 'today' . . . all gates, all doors, all arms are open to you while you're hot, but the day your show is cancelled your name is forgotten. You can be a star one minute with people bowing, scraping and straining to hear your every word, but after it's all over you can't get a soul to listen to you." It's not for nothing that Henry served the long years of apprenticeship in his profession. It is a craft which can bring rewards that truly are beyond anyone's wildest dreams, but the nightmare falls from grace take you equally far down again. Henry is well aware of the traps; he will not fall into them. "Self-respect is the cornerstone of joy," runs the text of one of Henry's favourite sayings. It's that same self-respect, tempered with a generous helping of self-awareness, that has brought Henry this far in his career and will undoubtedly take him further still.

One aspect of fame that he has had to come to

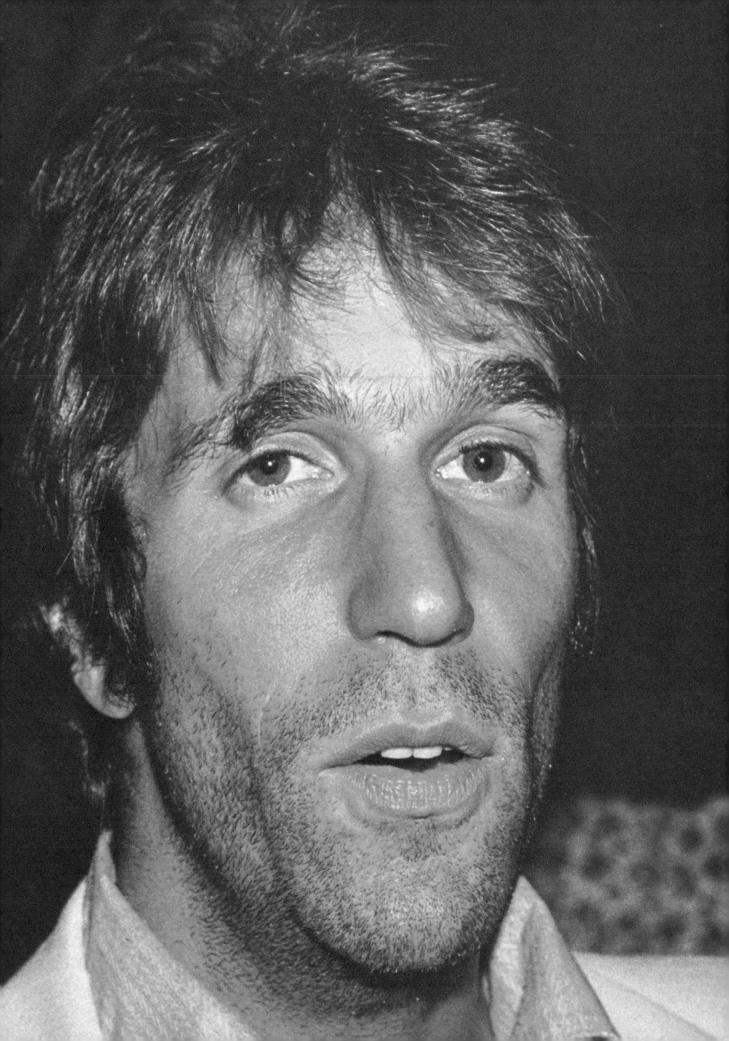

terms with is the whole problem of his audiences inevitably loving Fonzie rather than Henry. We've already mentioned how the thousands of letters to "Dear Fonzie" come into the ABC studios every week, how girls rush up to him on the street to cry "Fonzie! Fonzie!" and how their boyfriends wave their thumbs in the air and shout "Aaaaaayyy!!" whenever he passes by. Henry is conducting a one-man campaign to make sure that it's Winkler rather than Fonzarelli who hits the headlines, but even he must be delighted when certain aspects of the Fonz are brought to light.

"The most exciting thing about this whole experience is that my energy can touch so many different people, so many different ages. Isn't that what acting is all about: heightened communication?"

Henry is continually hearing reports about the effect that his "heightened communication" is having. One mother of a hyperactive child told him that watching Fonzie, and trying to imitate that very cool character, has calmed down her son in a way that drugs never could. You just can't be cool and hyperactive at the same time. Other stories tell how disabled children, delighted

Vietnam Veteran, Henry Winkler is lost for words when Sally Field pops out of his shower (A scene from Henry's film 'Heroes')

by the Fonz, have set out on a return to a normal life by copying Fonzie's thumbs-up signal. Children otherwise branded as "low achievers" have struggled heroically to pen letters to their hero. One New Jersey mental hospital administrator was so impressed by the positive effect *Happy Days* had on the viewing public that he has written in a medical journal saying just that. These kind of tributes don't come to just any star. It's a far cry from lipstick stained hankies or imploring letters of undying affection — the lot of any major media figure in these days of mass communication — to

these unstinting statements of the truly wonderful effect of a figure.

Henry has called *Happy Days* "a half-hour piece of fluff", but that piece of typically Winkleresque under-statement doesn't hold much water in the face of these honest testimonials. Nor when it comes up against the in-person experiences of Fonzie's power that Henry relates. He tells the story of his visit to a hospital for the disabled. There, amongst the most severely handicapped youngsters, Henry met a boy who was totally paralysed after a car crash at the age of nineteen. A full and active

life lay in ruins. The boy was utterly dejected, totally without will or strength. "The hand I took was lifeless, as I spoke to him his eyes just gazed at me blankly. Just as I was leaving I showed him the picture of the Fonz that I was going to sign and give to him. When he recognised it he started to get up from his bed!"

To turn from such wonderful stories to events of a more matter-of-fact, though equally important nature, it seems hardly any time since Henry Winkler was a regular star of not just the small screen, but also of those Hollywood gossip magazines that specialise in hot headlines and less than spectacular stories beneath them. With the kind of Neilsen ratings that would set any starlet's heart pounding, Henry was high up there on the list of eligible bachelors. Today Henry may have found the girl of his dreams — lovely Stacey Weitzman — but as those old gossips reveal, he didn't stint himself in his days as a bachelor. The thing was, and it's no surprise with Henry, that in his relationships as in his performance in a more

It's back
to the Men's Room
for Fonzie. Henry Winkler takes
care of business with Sally Field in his film 'Heroes'.

professional sphere, Henry demanded perfection. Mix his self-criticism with the long hard look that every new girlfriend had to undergo, and you don't exactly have the formula for long-standing relationships. Except of course when Ms Right turns up. Not that Henry wasn't attractive to women, and he certainly was partial to them. They just didn't seem to stay around that long. Maybe nice Jewish boys from New York City aren't cut out for the sultry Southern belles that Henry always seemed to fall for. And he didn't fare much better with the various starlets — from all over the States — with whom he was paired off in Hollywood. Stacey, on the other hand, apparently fits the bill most of the other women in Winkler's life never even wanted to read. "My relationship with Stacey is different from any other I've ever had in my life.

I'm very lucky. As frightening as an emotional relationship is, I cannot lie about this one. It's changed my life. Calmed me down."

Henry has fulfilled his three-year contract with *Happy Days*. He is looking forward to a new career out of television and in the movies. The world sits obediently at his feet and Henry knows that now, at least, all opportunities are his for the taking. "Life," he says, "is full of risks. You take them or you don't." To date, Henry has taken his share of risks and they've brought him an outsize helping of success, fortune and fame. The future is anyone's guess, though however much Henry may stress fame's here today, gone tomorrow quality, it would be a foolish person who tossed him aside as a one-role wonder. We can only wait and wonder.

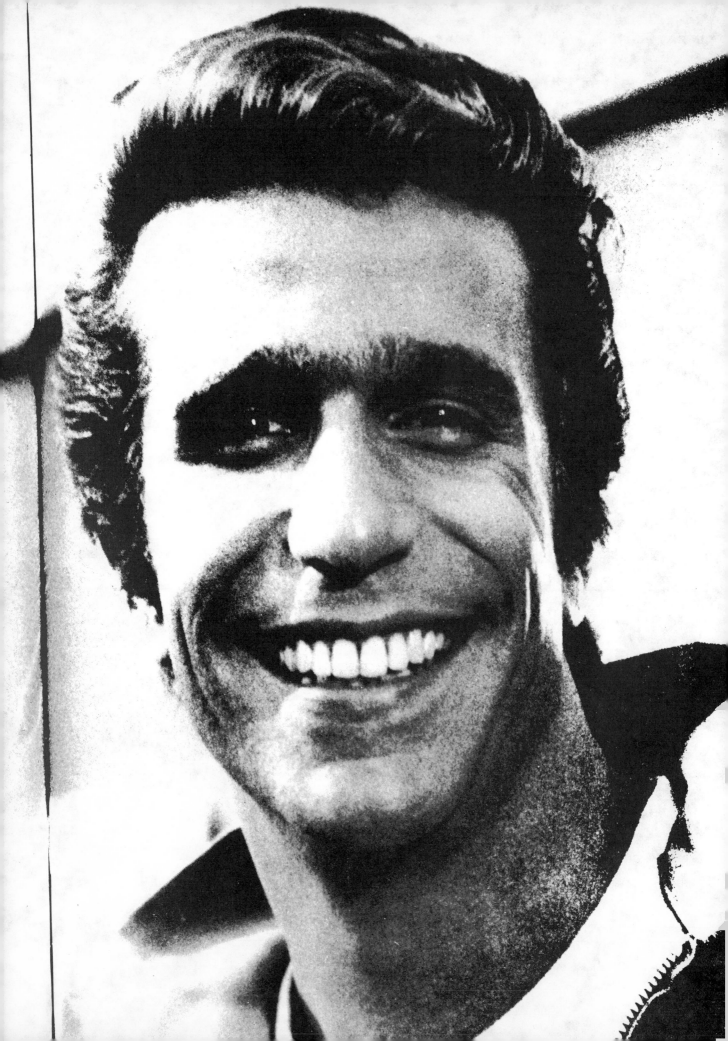